If the South
Had Won the Civil War

Forge Books by MacKinlay Kantor

Long Remember
If the South Had Won the Civil War

If the South Had Won the Civil War

MacKinlay Kantor

A Tom Doherty Associates Book
New York

IF THE SOUTH HAD WON THE CIVIL WAR

Copyright © 1960 by MacKinlay Kantor. Renewed © 1988 by the Estate of MacKinlay Kantor. Reprinted by permission of the Kantor Estate and the Estate's agent, Donald Maass, 157 West 57th Street, Suite 703, New York, NY 10019.

"An Historical Inversion," copyright © 1967 by MacKinlay Kantor. Renewed © 1995 by the Estate of MacKinlay Kantor. Reprinted by permission of the Kantor Estate and the Estate's agent, Donald Maass.

If the South Had Won the Civil War was first published in *Look* magazine in 1960, and, together with "An Historical Inversion," was included in *Story Teller*, published by Doubleday in 1967.

Introduction copyright © 2001 by Harry N. Turtledove

Interior illustrations copyright © 2001 by Dan Nance

Text design by Jane Adele Regina

A Forge Book
Published by Tom Doherty Associates, LLC
175 Fifth Avenue
New York, NY 10010

www.tor.com

Forge® is a registered trademark of Tom Doherty Associates, LLC.

Library of Congress Cataloging-in-Publication Data

Kantor, MacKinlay.
     If the South had won the Civil War / MacKinlay Kantor.
         p.   cm.
     Originally published in 1967 as a short story in the book Story Teller.
     "A Tom Doherty Associates book."
     ISBN 0-312-86553-8 (hc)
     ISBN 0-312-86949-5 (pbk)
        1. United States—History—Civil War, 1861–1865—Fiction.
        2. Southern States—Fiction.   I. Title.
PS3521.A47 I35   2001
813'.52—dc21   2001033518

First Forge Edition: November 2001

Printed in the United States of America

0   9   8   7   6   5   4   3   2   1

INTRODUCTION BY HARRY TURTLEDOVE

If the South Had Won the Civil War is, I think, the first work of alternate history I ever found. Almost forty years ago my ninth-grade English teacher kept a couple of shelves of paperbacks that her students could read if they finished assignments early—better that they read, she reasoned, than raise a ruckus, as ninth-graders with time on their hands are only too likely to do. Those shelves included out-and-out science fiction, which was plenty to lure me over: I remember an A. E. van Vogt novel and a Judith Merril year's-best anthology. And they also included *If the South Had Won the Civil War.*

MacKinlay Kantor's slim work of speculation was not presented as science fiction. I doubt that Kantor himself thought of it as science fiction; that was not where his main field of interest lay. He is best remembered today for *Andersonville,* arguably the greatest Civil War novel of all time, a harrowing, meticulously researched, and splendidly written tale of the Confederate prisoner-of-war camp in Georgia. But *Andersonville* is only the high point of a writing career that spanned more than half a century.

He began at seventeen, as a newspaperman on his hometown paper, the *Webster City* [Iowa] *Daily News* (the fact that his mother edited the *Daily News* probably didn't hurt). His first novel, *Diversey,* was published in 1928, when he was twenty-four. His first bestseller, *Long Remember,* came out in 1934. After Hollywood bought the rights to it, Kantor moved from Iowa to California to work as a screenwriter. During World War II, he was a correspondent covering the air war in the European theater. His 1945 novel, *Glory for Me*, was made into the film *The Best Years of Our Lives*. *Andersonville* appeared in 1955 and won the Pulitzer Prize for literature. Along with hundreds of short stories, articles, essays, and poems, Kantor published thirty-two books, the last of which, *Valley Forge*, appeared not long before his death in 1977.

The alternate world of *If the South Had Won the Civil War* departs from ours in two places in 1863: in the accidental death of Ulysses S. Grant during his advance upon Vicksburg and the disastrous failure of the campaign following his loss, and a Confederate victory at Gettysburg. Had these events turned out as Kantor described, there would be little doubt that the Confederate States would have won their independence on the battlefield.

Establishing the historical breakpoint (or, in this case, twin breakpoints) is only half the game of writing alternate history. The other half, and to me the more interesting one, is imagining what would spring from the proposed change. It is in that second half of the game that science fiction and alternate history come together. Both seek to extrapolate logically from a change in the world as we know it. Most forms of science fiction posit a change in the present or nearer future and imagine its effect on the more distant future. Alternate history, on the other hand, imagines a change in the more distant past and examines its consequences for the nearer past and the present. The technique is the same in both cases; the difference lies in where in time it is applied.

One of the amusing and enjoyable games the writer of alternate history can play is looking at the lives of prominent people under changed circumstances. For instance, what would Alexander the Great have done if his father, Philip of Macedon, hadn't been murdered in 336 BC? In more modern times, what sort of career would John F. Kennedy have had if he himself had escaped assassination in 1963?

Kantor plays this game as well as anyone. For example, at the time of the outbreak of the First World War, he imagines Theodore Roosevelt as President of the United States and Woodrow Wilson as President of the Confederate States (along with one Roy Smith as President of the Republic of Texas, which he envisions seceding from the CSA). The choices of Roosevelt and Wilson cannot, I think, be improved upon for dramatic potential at this crucial time in the history of America and of the world. That being so, I also used them as heads of the USA and CSA, respectively, in my own very different alternate World War I, the *Great War* series. Sometimes something seems so perfectly *right*, one has to use it even if it has been done before.

Many alternate histories are dystopias: they create worlds worse than our own and use them to point out our failings and foibles. The continued interest in books where the Axis won the Second World War (perhaps the finest of which, Philip K. Dick's *The Man in the High Castle*, appeared not long after *If the South Had Won the Civil War*) is a case in point. But Kantor's work is a genial exception to the rule. Written just before the centennial of the Civil War (it first ran in the November 22, 1960, issue of *Look*), it takes as its thesis that Americans would have stayed very much alike and maintain close ties to one another regardless of whether they chanced to live under the Stars and Stripes, the Stars and Bars, or the Lone Star Flag.

Is that true? Who knows? In any case, it's

the wrong question to ask of a work of alternate history. This is *fiction*, after all, and should be judged like any other piece of fiction. Is it entertaining? Is it plausible? Is it thought-provoking? Yes, on all three counts. For that reason, I am honored to have the privilege of writing this introduction and delighted that *If the South Had Won the Civil War* is back in print more than forty years after its original appearance.

IF THE SOUTH

HAD WON THE CIVIL WAR

The Past is immutable as such. Yet, in Present and in Future, its accumulated works can be altered by the whim of Time. . . .

As we enter the centennial of those military events which assured to the Confederate States of America their independence, it seems incumbent upon the historian to review a pageant bugled up from dusty lanes of the nineteenth century, to comment upon the actors appearing in such vast procession, and to inquire into the means by which they galloped toward fame or ignominy.

(If one would wish to apply this scrutiny to earlier epochs, he might in the same manner ask himself what would have befallen had winds not torn the canvas of the Spanish Armada?—had the Pilgrims landed on that Virginia coast for which they were originally primed?—had the boat bearing Washington capsized in the Delaware River?—had Pakenham been able to sweep triumphantly across the cotton-bale breastworks at New Orleans?)

Fruit of history contains many seeds of truth; yet unglimpsed orchards might have bloomed profusely in any season, were all the seeds planted and cultured before they dried past hope of germination.

Our American Civil War ended abruptly in July, 1863, with the shattering of the two most puissant armies which the North had been able to muster and marshal.

There was no more rebellion. Instead there *had been* a revolution, and the success of that enterprise now became assured—first, in Mississippi—and, almost simultaneously, some fourteen hundred miles away, among the green ridges which bend across the Pennsylvania-Maryland line.

The death of Major General U. S. Grant came as a sickening shock to those Northerners who had held high hopes for a successful campaign in the West—for the reduction of Port Hudson and Vicksburg, and the freeing of the Mississippi River from Confederate domination.

Monumental effects of the catastrophe (Grant's death) could not be observed for nearly seven weeks, such was the confusion of operations within the State of Mississippi.

The fatal accident befell in the late afternoon of Tuesday, May 12th, 1863, on a narrow road winding among hills of Hinds County, Mississippi. (This was some forty-eight hours after Lieutenant General "Stonewall" Jackson breathed his last, in distant Virginia, and while officials and supporters of the National Government were still swallowing the acid of Chancellorsville.)

Grant had left Grand Gulf on May 7th, deliberately cutting himself off from his base of supplies. He fared into the field with only the barest staples for those three army corps under his command, and with problems of transport to be solved by the acquisition of civilian vehicles. His projected march might have been considered Napoleonic in its conception and in its rashness, though future historians would censure Grant for having projected a suicidal venture. It must be remembered, however, that the springtime campaign had thus far moved with celerity. Union gunboats and steamers had successfully run the blockade at Vicksburg on the moonless night of April 16th; and Grant had marched his troops across a vast western bend of the Mississippi, in order to be picked up by the fleet—below Vicksburg, far out of interference by Confederate batteries—and transported to the east bank of the Mississippi River.

Lieutenant General John Pemberton, venturing out from the defenses of Vicksburg, was still mainly inactive. General Joseph E. Johnston had not yet assumed command of the Confederate forces at and near Jackson. Grant was now pressing his advance through unoccupied country between two hostile armies. But he had left himself with no vulnerable rear for Pemberton to fall upon.

Grant was traditionally given to taciturnity and self-consultation. No one knows exactly what was in his mind. It is believed that he intended to throw himself against Jackson, capture the State capital, and cut the railroad leading from Jackson to Vicksburg, thus depriving the besieged river bastion of any possibility for supply or reinforcement.

On May 12th, the Union advance had pressed beyond Fourteen Mile Creek. Major General John A. McClernand's Corps was moving on the left, with its flank held firmly against the Big Black River. By late afternoon McClernand had shoved across Fourteen Mile Creek; his pickets were within two miles of Edwards Station on the Vicksburg & Jackson Railroad. Major General Wm. T. Sherman held the center of the northward-turning Union advance. Major General James B. McPherson held the right. That afternoon elements of McPherson's Corps encountered the Confederate Brigadier General Gregg, with a moderate force, near Raymond. Major General John A. Logan's Division attacked speedily, and, after a brief but spirited encounter, nullified the Confederate resistance and sent Gregg in rapid retreat.

Orders for the next day, for specific movements on specific roads, had already been issued. Then Grant received his despatch from McPherson, telling of McPherson's successful drive upon Raymond.

Many historians believe that decisively Grant might have altered his plans for movements on the 13th, had he lived a little longer.

Grant was accompanying the command of his admired and admiring "Cump" Sherman. In addition to his regular staff, Grant had in his peripatetic military household his son Frederick, twelve years of age. There was also present the journalist, Mr. Charles A. Dana, later named to be Assistant Secretary of War.

A few days afterward Dana wrote to a friend: "General Grant took the despatch and read it twice. He did not immediately discuss the contents of the note with anyone, but this was not unusual. He pocketed the envelope; there was a look of satisfaction on his face. He was mounted when he received the despatch, and remained in his saddle throughout the reading."

Two of Grant's favorite steeds had gone lame. Grant was riding a fractious horse, one which his groom had not wished him to ride. But the general, a master of equitation, would not brook the delay necessary to the finding of another mount. He had ridden the big chestnut since noon, although frequently he was observed as having difficulty in keeping the beast under control.

There was the usual coterie of lookers-on present in the neighborhood: gaunt farm boys, little girls, a few Negroes. These clung in fence corners or at crossroads, glowering or looking gleeful or merely awed, as is the habit of civilians in an area traversed by armies.

Grant's horse first became unsettled because of the blast of a whistle from Fairchild's steam mill, located nearby. There was a head of steam up in the boiler. It was said later that the first officers who moved in the advance wished steam to be kept up in the mill for some military purpose. This was never explained. But when a foolish blast from the whistle ensued, Grant's horse was seen to grow increasingly nervous.

Edward H. Sittenfield, later U.S. senator

from Illinois and then serving as a staff major,
writes:*

"I had noticed that a little girl was huddled
on a rail fence, holding a cat wrapped in a shawl
in her lap. Perhaps Kitty scratched the child.
At any rate she dropped the cat, and the next
moment it was pursued by a large white-and-
tan hound. The speeding animals dashed across
the roadway directly in front of Grant's horse.
Someone cried out, so we all turned. There were
many witnesses to this occurrence."

Grant's mount rose tall upon its hind legs,
then flung itself to one side with a desperate
whinny. No horseman in the world could have
held his seat in such a shying. Even as it reared
the horse lost footing in the clay road and
pitched heavily to one side, landing half on its
back, with the rider underneath, receiving the
weight of the crushing flailing body.

There was also the matter of the rock: a
fair-sized whitish stone, washed out from clay
at that point. Some witnesses insist that Grant's

---

*My Service In Saddle and In Senate, by Edward
Harkins Sittenfield. (Boston). Houghton, Mifflin Co.
1904.

head struck the rock—there was blood upon the stone when they removed the fallen general. Others give contrary information. But whatever his injuries, and however received, the commander of the Army of the Tennessee now lay unconscious. The horse was writhing, inflicting fresh injuries upon the recumbent body beneath it at every move.

A young staff captain, Hubert Gaines, had the presence of mind to swing from his horse and run forward, drawing his revolver in the same moment. He fired two shots into the animal's ear and the great beast lay still. Then Grant could be removed—his uniform covered with clay, and blood issuing from his nose and mouth. Mr. Charles A. Dana himself escorted the white-faced little Frederick Grant away.

Ulysses Grant spoke no coherent word. As people placed him tenderly upon a hastily-improvised couch of blankets his respiration was labored and his pulse weak. A surgeon was found (after some fifteen minutes, during which time others tried to render what aid they could). When he arrived the surgeon pronounced Grant dead.

Sittenfield writes feelingly: "Another month, another hour, another place? What might have been the historical residue? Suppose, let us say, that General Grant had never suffered such an accident until after the termination of his Mississippi campaign. We cannot help but hold that, with his presence and guiding direction and genius, there would have been a far different result to that same campaign. Let us suppose further that a shying horse had fallen upon him three months later—perhaps in August, perhaps not in the field, but in a region won by the investment of Federal arms, and saved by the application of Grant's own genius. What would the result have been? It would have been negative, it might in no way have affected the immediate conduct of the war. Only in the long view would this same tragedy have obtained. Let us suppose still further, perhaps, that the fall did not result fatally. A few painful weeks in bed, and then up and about on crutches, and returning eventually to active command in the field! Ah, the great chargers of history pass before us now, from Bucephalus on to George Washington's famous Blueskin; and the fractious chestnut ridden by U. S. Grant on May 12, 1863, takes a shamed place in the rearguard!"

McClernand ranked both W. T. Sherman and J. B. McPherson, and on his arrogant shoulders there now fell a mantle which draped him almost ludicrously.

The speed and agility of the Army of the Tennessee was departed—it might have oozed away in the last outpouring of Ulysses Grant's blood.

Either of the two West Pointers would have been far more fitted to command; but the distant Halleck (despite his dislike for McClernand) was never a man to slice sharply to the quick of a matter. Nor, it must be confessed, was Abraham Lincoln, especially where one of his own military appointments was concerned. That pompous unruly Illinois politician, John A. McClernand, had been given his commission originally because he was a Democratic congressman—from Lincoln's own district—who had been the Chief Executive's friend before the war, and remained his supporter in time of later argument and peril. The friendship of Democratic congressmen to the war effort was needed sorely—and perhaps, Lincoln appeared to believe, in the army as well. McClernand was a cackling middle-aged chicken who had come home to roost.

Despite Grant's removal from existence, and subsequent military misfortunes resulting to the Unionists, their campaign so auspiciously begun might still have been concluded successfully had the Confederate President and his two field commanders, Johnston and Pemberton, descended into contradiction and confusion. Joseph E. Johnston, plagued by dysentery, and suffering still from severe wounds received in 1862, made record speed when ordered from Tullahoma to Jackson. Having arrived at the Mississippi capital and become familiar with the situation, he ordered Pemberton to move on Clinton immediately, with the intention of sweeping aside any Federal troops in his path and effecting a juncture with the Southern reinforcements hastening toward Jackson.

President Jefferson Davis, previously committed to an opinion that Pemberton should retain the bulk of his army in the Vicksburg area, was now converted to Johnston's belief: i.e., that a general engagement with the Northerners, if delayed until a juncture of Confederate arms was completed, might (as Davis wrote later) "render retreat or reinforcement to the enemy scarcely practicable." Pemberton, capricious and stubbornly assertive prior to that hour, responded to Johnston's orders with alacrity.

An abortive attack on the city of Jackson, a delayed attempt to cut the railroad near Clinton, the final debacle at Champion's Hill: these were as much—or even more—a result of bad generalship on the Union side as they were of the wisdom of Johnston's over-all strategy and Pemberton's willingness to comply. Federal forces were depleted almost daily—frittered away in costly battles which should have been mere touch-and-go skirmishes. The slightest penetration of strong Confederate defenses seemed, to McClernand, sufficient excuse to throw in a few brigades in a foolish attempt to hold and solidify a position palpably untenable in the end.

Quickly the problem of supply became

acute: the Federals were starving in the field. When at last the citizen-soldier had exhibited his faults in repeated demonstrations sufficient for even a Halleck to understand, it was too late for Sherman, the new commander, to salvage even a crumb of victory. The Northerners must seek their supply lines again or they would perish where they stood.

Humiliated and embittered, Sherman withdrew to the Mississippi, with Logan's Division of the Seventeenth Corps sacrificing heavily in a rearguard action which insured the escape of the main columns. A month to the day from that May 7th when U. S. Grant, living and intent, had cut loose from Grand Gulf, the retreating Army of the Tennessee was back on the banks of the big river—mauled, hungry, and the poorer by at least twelve thousand casualties.

Through the hot month of June the star of the Confederates scintillated into a new ascendancy, the star of the North declined. Doggedly Sherman clung to that belief he embraced the year before, and which also had been a conviction of the now-vanished Grant: Vicksburg could be reduced only by a land army operating from the land, and any attack by naval vessels would be fruitless. Still, if Sherman were to achieve a satisfactory base on the high ground of Walnut Hills, north of Vicksburg, he must in effect reverse his field, ferry across the Mississippi once more, and return to Milliken's Bend, and, eventually, to the east shore. This was the movement carried out; but in a fatal midnight the steamers which sought to run up the river past Vicksburg were not charmed as they seemed to have been when they puffed south in April. Vessel after vessel was set afire or sunk by Confederate batteries. Strangely enough this disaster occurred only a few hours before Major General Nathaniel P. Banks made his ill-conceived assault on the works at Port Hudson, in Louisiana, to be thrown back with appalling waste.

On Friday, June 26th, Sherman, reinforced at last by the survivors of Banks' command, had recrossed the Mississippi and was in position for the assault. Percentage-wise, the Army of the Tennessee then suffered the most severe losses of any command, North or South, during the war. Five hours after the initial attack was launched, Union regiments were being commanded by lieutenants, army divisions by colo-

nels; and there had ensued no permanent breach of the Confederate works. The next day Johnston crossed the Big Black River; Sunday afternoon he fell upon the Federal flank and rear. (During the first hour of Johnston's attack, J. B. McPherson, a future President of the United States, was seriously wounded.) On Monday morning Pemberton sallied forth from Vicksburg, and the Army of the Tennessee was trapped against the Mississippi shore. The surrender came on Tuesday, the last day of a miserable month for the Federals.

William Tecumseh Sherman was not present to deliver the surrender. The turbulent but dedicated commander risked fire once too often. An anonymous sharpshooter had drilled his red head the previous afternoon.

It is not likely that one in a hundred either of the defeated or the victorious troops at Vicksburg had ever heard of another *burg*: a place called Gettysburg.

Nor was the name of that little Pennsylvania town commonly recognized by people in the

Army of the Potomac, or in the Army of Northern Virginia. Those soldiers learned about Gettysburg (many of them to their dismay or extinction) on July 1st, while the once proud Army of the Tennessee was still signing its parole beside the Mississippi.

There could be little purpose in reciting in detail the events of that first day's battle. A fumbling encounter near Willoughby Run before the sun was high—the rush of the Union First Corps into battle against Lieutenant General A. P. Hill, the death of Major General John F. Reynolds, a hasty forward movement of the Union Eleventh Corps, the jar as Lieutenant General Richard S. Ewell struck them, the dissolution of the Federal lines at mid-afternoon— These are matters of common knowledge.

But what is not realized too generally is the fact that, despite the flight of disordered Federal forces through the village of Gettysburg, despite their heavy loss in prisoners, despite a solely precarious hold which elements of the First and Eleventh Corps obtained on the Cemetery Hill south of town— Despite these gains, it would have been wholly possible for General Robert E. Lee to have lost the battle or to have *begun* losing it, about five P.M. that afternoon.

Many of Lee's biographers believe that the events of the next hour went as far toward altering the course of America's history as any single hour might go.

Lee's attitude was a marvel to those about him. He was decisive, incisive; and the orders which he issued brooked no misinterpretation. Colonel Kenneth Reidun-Clarke, who was an observer in the field and later wrote a definitive history of the War for Southern Independence,* says: "In many previous circumstances which might be considered similar, there had been a tendency toward ambiguity manifest in General Lee. This I did not observe to be the case at Gettysburg. He said quietly: 'The enemy is there, and I will attack him now.' Frequently it seemed that I had detected in the orders issued by Lee to his subordinates an over-willingness to allow those subordinates to exercise their own discretion. Had, for instance, the commander of the Army of Northern Virginia suggested to Ew-

---

The War of the American Secession. Kenneth Reidun-Clarke, C.B. (New York). The Century Company. 1888.

ell that he should attack the Federals in their new position *only if it seemed to him to be practicable, or only if in considered judgment he felt it wise,* there might have been a different story to relate, and quite another ending to the battle at Gettysburg. But this was not the case: no one could have misunderstood the desires of Lee. He wished to press an advantage already gained, and would not be deterred."

Ewell's Corps, having joined battle much later than Hill's, was infinitely fresher. Brigadier General Alfred Iverson's and Brigadier General Junius Daniel's brigades moved rapidly to the base of Cemetery Hill, where they encountered the ineffectual fire of a Yankee skirmish line. These skirmishers had been thrown out only a few minutes earlier by Major General W. S. Hancock, who had just arrived on the hill, far in advance of his own Second Corps (and was instructed by Meade to survey the situation).

Hancock announced to Major General Oliver Howard that he would assume command; but met with objections of the Eleventh Corps Commander, who insisted that he was the senior in rank. Hancock then replied that he would leave at once and make a personal report to Ma-

jor General George G. Meade. But Howard was reluctant to agree to this also, declaring: "I need you here to assist in forming these lines."

In soldierly manner Hancock agreed, and endeavored to bring order out of chaos. He might indeed have succeeded in his efforts had Ewell delayed in attacking the hill. Hancock threw out a skirmish line (as noted in the foregoing) and also attempted to establish a brigade on Culp's Hill on the Union right.

The demoralization of the Union forces was so acute that Hancock met with great difficulty in identifying or assembling a full brigade for this purpose. Thus a random selection of broken and disorganized regiments, including troops of both the First and the Eleventh Corps, were told off for this task and moved at once toward Culp's Hill.

They had but entered the valley lying between the two eminences when they were struck on their left by Major General Jubal A. Early's Division. Simultaneously, on the Confederate right, Major General W. D. Pender's Division of Hill's Corps moved against the west slope of the Cemetery Hill, Brigadier General Samuel McGowan's and Brigadier General Alfred M. Scales' brigades leading on. This was an attack of Carolinians almost without exception, save for the crushing assault by Early on the Confederate left.

Already the Confederate artillery was shelling roads behind the cemetery, and inflicting casualties on advance elements of the Union Twelfth Corps, who were just moving in from Littlestown. The feeble and exhausted lines of skirmishers were slain, captured or overrun within a matter of minutes, and Major General Robt. E. Rode's and Pender's Divisions forced their way triumphantly into the cemetery. Fierce hand-to-hand fighting raged among the tombstones. But the issue could no longer be in doubt: the battered Eleventh Corps—or rather the survivors of that much-mauled organization—gave way rapidly, and blundered toward the rear in a panic not unlike that endured at Chancellorsville.

Even at this late hour the heat of the day was exhausting, both to attackers and defenders; but the morale of the victorious Confederates seemed to be giving them an added transfusion of vigor.

Long before dusk, Ewell, together with

Pender's Division, was firmly established on both the Cemetery Hill and Culp's Hill. The remnants of the right wing of the Army of the Potomac stumbled in flight down the Baltimore Pike or along the road leading south to Taneytown.

Lee had ridden out of town to his right, in order to observe the battle more clearly. A report reached him that Hancock had just been captured, seriously wounded. "See that he is made as comfortable as possible," Lee instructed an orderly, and then he took up his glasses for another examination of the field. He lowered the glasses. Colonel Reidun-Clarke insists that Lee said quietly, as if to himself, "I didn't know Dick Ewell could move so rapidly."

A noted historian of the Southern Revolution, H. H. Pettigrew* (1870–1946: son of Johnston Pettigrew, a Confederate general officer) has examined those elements

---

*The Last Campaign. H. H. Pettigrew. (Charleston, S. C.). John Zacharias & Co. 1921.

contributing to the success of the Confederates at Gettysburg and during the battles which followed as victorious gray armies thundered once more into Maryland. Pettigrew considers the fact that Lee observed the importance of two hills at the southern prolongation of the Cemetery Ridge—i.e., Little Round Top and Round Top—and immediately gave orders for their occupation, to be a positive circumstance in the determination of a Confederate victory. This was the entering wedge by which Lee drove his forces between scattered Union army corps and sent them sprawling.

But almost of equal effect might be considered the shrewdness and audacity displayed by Major General J. E. B. Stuart in flinging his cavalry against Major General Alfred Pleasanton's cavalry in the early morning of July 2nd. A less able general might have ignored Pleasanton's very existence, after a preliminary brush with the Federal cavalry on the outskirts of Hanover two days earlier. If Stuart had progressed northeasterly toward York, or perhaps northwesterly in the direction of Carlisle, the Army of Northern Virginia would have been bereft of his services at a time when they were needed urgently. With Pleasanton's forces mainly scattered and reeling in defeat, Stuart achieved his first contact with the bulk of the Confederate Army since he left Virginia.

Equally dramatic, if not equally decisive, was the forced march made from the Chambersburg region by Major General George E. Pickett's Division of Lieutenant General James Longstreet's Corps, and the introduction—after a much-needed few hours of sleep—of a large body of fresh troops unwearied by participation in previous fighting. Also there must be taken into consideration the indecisiveness of General Meade, and the poor staff work which ruled: corps commanders not knowing the location of other corps—uncertainty about the choosing of defensive positions—an utter lack of intercommunication and liaison among the Federal units.

With both the Taneytown road and the Emmitsburg road tightly in his grasp, Lee mauled his way down into Maryland, crushing the Northern forces in detail. After a single bitter and bloody encounter, Major General Daniel E. Sickles managed to escape with the greater portion of his Third Corps, and swing rapidly to the

East; but most other bodies of National troops were not so fortunate.

Stuart's cavalry deployed to attack Federal elements from the rear, and became an integral factor in the demolishing of the Union Second Corps. In piecemeal fashion, the Union Fifth and Sixth Corps were broken to bits before they could assume proper defensive positions on Pipe Creek; nor could they effectually unite with the survivors of proceeding battles.

By sunset on July 3rd, the Army of the Potomac had dissolved into hopeless tatters—bleeding human garbage, a pitiful mockery of an army. Brigade after brigade was cut off. Many surrendered intact; others, resisting frantically, and often without sufficient ammunition, were annihilated. Lee attempted to appeal to Meade for a surrender which would bring an end to this slaughter; but he had much difficulty in communicating with the Union commander, or even in discovering his whereabouts. It was the saddest Fourth of July in United States history.

Panic ruled in Philadelphia, Baltimore, in New York City, and, of course, in Washington. News of the military tragedies which had affected the National Government in two widely-separated areas, plunged the entire North into either hysteria or paralysis. In Baltimore and New York, as well as in Chicago, droves of hoodlums—professing Southern sympathies, but impelled principally by a desire for anarchistic saturnalia—seized the city offices. They looted and burned at will, and were routed only when Federal troops moved against them with artillery.

This was not merely defeat. It was a disaster of such magnitude that many Southern leaders pleaded for a compassion which would not make America into an object of disgust and derision before the civilized world.

In Washington, the so-called contrabands, who had drifted into the District of Columbia region as a result of the war, and who dwelt in the new Arlington camp or were employed in the capital—These colored unfortunates rioted past the unsteady troops who guarded them, attempting to flee, they knew not where. Rumors of "slave insurrection" and "black rebellionists" fluttered through the streets, and here again the criminal element achieved mastery. Not only in Washington, but in other principal cities

throughout the North, hundreds of Negroes were hounded through the alleys, had their brains bashed out by cobblestones, were hanged, burned, torn to pieces, just as rapidly as they fell into the hands of maniacal mobs. Not only the army, not only the structure of government, but the soul and body of the Nation seemed to be falling apart.

July turned unseasonably chilly following torrential rains in the Washington, D.C. region on the 3rd and 4th.

By Monday evening, Ward Hill Lamon, the President's close personal friend, and Marshal of the District of Columbia, was obsessed by fears for Mr. Lincoln's safety. Twice during the day lawless crowds had endeavored to storm into the White House, and were driven back by bayonets of the infantry on guard.

Lamon himself disappeared from the scene before sunset, and did not return for nearly three hours. A rumor had reached him and he wanted to explore it.

When Lamon returned to the White House, where he had been in residence since the first news of military calamities arrived (each night he had slept with loaded pistols beside him, on a rug outside the President's door), he was accompanied by half a dozen horsemen who wore mackintosh capes over their other clothing. The little cavalcade was followed closely by a large van used for delivery of ice during the summer months; but two New York cavalrymen occupied the driver's seat.

Marshal Lamon entered the White House, while his unidentified companions waited in shadows outside the west door. According to a later statement made by the marshal, he found President Lincoln lying on a sofa, sole alone, in the darkened East Room. The President had a severe headache, and a damp handkerchief was folded across his eyes.

Lamon's first words brought Abraham Lincoln to his feet. "You shan't stay here an hour longer! I can't be responsible for your safety if you remain—no one could."

The President smiled bleakly. "Just where might we go? The railroads to the North are cut, and you tell me that all of Maryland is in revolt."

"True, true," cried Lamon impatiently, "but I have other plans for you."

"Well, Hill, I have news for you as well: I am going no place."

The mighty Lamon took a deep breath. "You will go if I have to pick you up in my arms and carry you. Go—if I have to clout you over the head and render you unconscious! I have already informed Mrs. Lincoln and Bob, and they're preparing for a journey. If you persist in being stubborn," Lamon finally exploded, "you'll have to answer to her, as well as to me."

Lamon said later that the President made his way upstairs without another word. Lamon watched him go, then hastened outside to make arrangements.

Raggle-taggle throngs were still clustered beyond the fence north of the White House, facing Lafayette Park. From the park itself rose the scream and mumble of crowds surrounding a couple of speakers who ranted on barrelheads in the glow of torchlight.

Lamon personally superintended the removal of some settees and hassocks, which were placed in the back of the ice-van. Then he reached the stairway in time to meet Mrs. Lincoln, who came down, sobbing wildly, with ten-year-old Tad clinging to her. Several servants carried a mass of luggage. Lamon knew well enough that there would be no room for such weighty impedimenta; but, in the wisdom of long experience, he said nothing to the President's wife. He drew her maid aside and ordered that only the most necessary bags be carried out. Robert Lincoln came from his room a moment later and escorted his weeping mother and little brother to the west door.

Lamon stood waiting for the President. When Mr. Lincoln appeared he was wearing a shabby old overcoat and toying with a crushed felt hat which he held in his hands.

"Hill," he said to Lamon, "remember how I wore these duds when I came into Washington, before the Inauguration?"

"I do indeed, sir. And I'm glad to see that you're no longer resisting my efforts for your safety and the safety of your family."

Lincoln walked slowly toward the west door. He repeated, as it were a litany: "I wore these duds when I came to Washington, and I might as well wear them going out."

Mrs. Lincoln and the boys were already in the van. The President halted a moment on the step and gazed sadly about, taking in the big wagon with its closed body, and the strange figures of mackintosh-draped horsemen alongside.

"Mr. President," said Lamon, joining him on the steps, "I have an introduction to perform." At his words one of the strangers stepped forward.

"Permit me, Mr. President, to introduce Major John Singleton Mosby of the Confederate States Army. He has very kindly expressed his willingness to accompany us, and I feel that we are in good custody."

The President shook hands with the young guerrilla leader. "Oh, yes," he said, but still speaking as if in a dream. "Mosby. Indeed I have heard of you."

Only after he was in the van and established on a settee opposite his wife, did he inquire of Lamon: "Just where are we bound?"

"To Richmond, Mr. President. I think 'twill be the safest place for you and the folks."

Lincoln made no reply, but reached across and stroked the head of the frightened Tad. Then he quoted in a dry whisper: "It is finished."

Major Mosby came to the rear of the van to assure the Lincolns that the furniture had been lashed firmly into place, and they need have no fear of an upset. The van began to move. It went rumbling out into 17th Street,

with Lamon and Mosby and five of Mosby's men riding in escort.

There were cat-calls, then a faint cheer from some of the disorderly rovers in the street, then sounds of a fist-fight breaking out. Several young men started at a dog-trot, following the van; but they fell back when two of the Confederate troopers halted and swung their mounts about to face them.

The fleeing party turned, moved east through the President's Park, crossed 15th Street, and turned south to reach the Long Bridge by a devious route. When they were a few blocks away from the White House, they met only with casually curious stares from people encountered.

Lamon had planned this flight adroitly and under pressure. He had learned that Stuart's cavalry were closing in north of the city, eager to be the first Confederate troops to enter the Nation's capital. But the slightly built Partisan Ranger had come on into town in advance, with a few of his men: a characteristic act in one who had explored the route for Stuart's famous Ride-around-McClellan the year before.

On reaching the Virginia side of the Potomac, the two Federal troopers got down from the wagon (they had no wish to go to Richmond!) and their places were taken by two of Mosby's men. Mosby led the party on south, bent on avoiding Alexandria by traveling on back roads which he knew so well.

It was typical of Mosby that he should be the first of the victorious soldiery to arrive in the Nation's capital; but the Partisan Rangers were followed quickly by other cavalry. Within a few hours after the flight of the Lincoln family, miscellaneous Confederates were prowling the White House corridors, or staring with awe into dark and silent chambers of House and Senate in the new Capitol building. There was no destruction and no wholesale looting by the military, although a good many souvenirs seemed to have been carried off during the first day or two of the Secessionists' occupancy. Items such as gavels, ink-stands, sofa-pillows and oil paintings had a way of turning up pridefully in Southern homes for some decades to come.

Still the only widespread pillaging, with its attendant cruelty, was charged to the mobs of citizenry. Loudly professing Southern sympathies, and rejoicing drunkenly in the downfall of the North, these wolf-packs stampeded up and down the streets, breaking into shops, setting fire or attempting to set fire to the houses of United States Government officials, mutilating stray Negroes, kidnapping prostitutes and sober housewives alike, and perpetrating every other manner of atrocity in the human decalogue. Although they might deplore such occurrences, the first few Confederate officers to reach the capital were powerless in the face of such widespread lunacy. Only artillery might have controlled those herds; and artillery could not be employed for fear of inflicting heavy casualties upon the thousands of bewildered men, women and children who huddled in their homes.

With dawn, July 7th, arrived the bulk of Jeb Stuart's command, and the worst was over. Daylight also revealed the National Colors floating over Government buildings, where they had been left through the days and nights preceding. Jaunty troopers immediately began hauling down the flags and substituting Confederate guidons or battle-banners. Such demonstrations of exuberance were halted in short order when General Lee and his staff reached Washington the next day. One of Lee's first orders dealt with the display of the United States flag.

"This is the capital of a Nation," he said. "It is a Nation of which we were once a part. It should be repugnant to any soldier of the Army of Northern Virginia to visit uncalled-for humiliation upon a brave, if humbled, foe. I desire earnestly that the Colors of the United States Government be restored to their rightful place until such time as the mediations of regularly constituted authorities may make other dispositions."

The weary commander of a victorious army quartered himself on that first night, and thereafter, in his old home: Arlington, on the hill beyond the Potomac. Mrs. Lee came to join him within the week.

However much Lee and others—North and South—might have desired those "regularly constituted authorities" to sit as a peace commission, and immediately, it was the middle of September before representatives of the two governments met in their historic conclave.

Meanwhile Federal troops finally brought order to the cities, expediting the martial law which prevailed almost throughout the Union. At first the status of the Presidency itself was in grave doubt. Who indeed *was* President of the United States? Was it Lincoln, who had fled to Richmond (or *deserted* to the Confederate cause, as his enemies proclaimed)? Or was it Hannibal Hamlin, formerly Vice-President, now automatically in succession? Even members of the Supreme Court were divided in their opinions. Indeed there were almost as many opinions as there were editors (once the process of the press was restored) or orators eager to prate from rostrum or wagon-tail.

The most puzzling aspects of the situation were dispelled on the receipt of a letter of resignation, unquestionably valid, from Mr. Lincoln himself. He addressed the Congress and the people of the United States at large.

"In the hallowed year of Seventeen-seventy-six," he wrote, "our fathers established, before the eyes of the world, a new Nation. But it now appears that Divine wisdom has dictated that that Nation shall henceforth be in twain."

Abraham Lincoln went on to acknowledge

that the military events of recent date had demonstrated that the United States of America could no longer be held together by force of arms. He tendered his formal resignation from the Presidency.

"Let Americans all," he said, "North and South, blue and gray, now affirm that our respective dead shall not have perished without purpose. Let us pray that our two governments shall have a new birth in freedom."

Mr. Lincoln's last word was interpreted variously by newspapers and statesmen alike. On the whole the public reaction was anything but complimentary, except in the case of the few fanatical devotees who never believed that Lincoln could commit an error. As for the ex-President himself, he had been invited to take up quarters in President Davis's mansion, once he was escorted to Richmond by Mosby. To be a guest in the home of the Secessionist President was not, however, to Mr. Lincoln's liking; although he was willing that his family should be cared for, politely if austerely, by their late enemies.

"No, Mr. Davis," Lamon recalls Lincoln's saying flatly to the Confederate dignitary, "it's just a case of which pen you happen to drive the calf into. Now, if you'd come our way, I suppose the public would have demanded that I put you in the Old Capitol prison. So pray to make whatever substitution for that famous edifice you can manage! Hill, please affirm to Mr. Jefferson Davis the fact that you would have clapped him in irons, had he ventured into your bailiwick."

"Not irons, sir," Lamon remonstrated, turning to Davis, "but I would have been compelled to incarcerate you."

Davis shrugged. "Let it be as you say."

Thereupon a section of Castle Thunder was vacated and scrubbed, and Abraham Lincoln was established there. Lamon wished to share his imprisonment.

"I am a Virginian by birth," he declared, "and, as such, I demand the right to accompany the President of the United States into exile, into a dungeon, or to the scaffold itself!"

It was decided that Lamon's status as Marshal of the District of Columbia was sufficient to allow him to become a prisoner of State. He was ensconced in a cell adjacent to that of Mr. Lincoln. Lamon's role became that of a glorified

secretary who spent most of his time acting as a bulwark between Abraham Lincoln and those who desired to see him, either to revile or—in some rare cases—to commiserate.

While Lincoln lived behind bars, the scissors of History and of Fate slashed at the map of the United States.

There sounded still the chatter of musketry, the pounding of cannon. A simultaneous collapse and defeat of the two stoutest armies which the North had put into the field was not accepted as *prima facie* evidence of a National surrender by certain doughty commanders whose far-flung forces still resisted. Men died during July, hopelessly or with supreme dedication, at lonely places in Arkansas, West Virginia, and in the South Central States. But the scale of the Confederacy had hurled itself aloft, the pan of the Union struck the ground with a disheartening thud.

In the general disorganization of government and of the military establishment, there could be no efficient supply or reinforcement of those units not directly affected by the obliteration of armies at Vicksburg and in the East. No one could count or name the last shot fired in a pitched battle, but certainly it spoke its echo into the hot air before the end of July. And, long since, the State of Maryland (following the brutal assassination of pro-Union Governor Augustus W. Bradford) had elected to join the Southern Confederacy—to be followed, in opinion and action, by Kentucky only five days later.

The loss of these two States did not come as a surprise to most of the North. It was recognized that Maryland and Kentucky had sent huge bodies of troops to support the Confederate arms. The delighted Secessionists contended spiritedly that neither State truly desired to remain as part of the Yankee structure, but had been held there either by trickery or by force.

Missouri, however, was quite another matter. Here there extended no Mason and Dixon line, nor was the Ohio River flowing within Missouri's boundaries. Truly the Missouri River did flow there, but its demarkation was neither geographical nor soundly political. A preponderance of Confederate sentiment bulked heavily in the northern counties: Sterling Price, the Marmadukes, Claiborne Fox Jackson and their adherents all came from that region. The mass of pro-Yankee sentiment was in the southern portion of the State—in the highlands, with the highlanders' traditional adherence to the *status quo* and their disinclination to change. Also there existed a solid core of pro-Nationalist sympathy among the Germans in St. Louis (a sturdy factor in the original decision that Missouri should remain with the North).

Kansas was no problem: a blanket of National troops had taken care of that; the Kansas question *per se* was long since solved. But the "bleeding Kansas" of yore found a counterpart in the "murderous Missouri" of the several months following July. From the leaders of both Confederate and United States governments issued appeals for tolerance, human sympathy, human decency. It was no more feasible for Federal troops to attempt upholding a northern Missouri regime by the strength of bayonets, than it was for the Confederate States' Government to send a punitive expedition through the Ozarks; though both courses were advocated by firebrands of either camp. Vicious raids by irresponsible freebooters did nothing to help the situation, no more than did the duels (these were a momentary disgrace): duels fought, many of them, by men prominent in the life of the State.

In the autumn, however, the State Legislature, which could by no stretch of imagination be called a rump, established Missouri's adherence to the North beyond any shadow of a doubt. Then, as in 1861, an official appeal was made for Federal troops. These were forthcoming, and remained on guard until 1866.

The Confederacy had little desire to expend blood in order to add doubtful territory to its possessions, when such rich and populous commonwealths as Kentucky and Maryland had swept into the Southern ranks without coercion. The pro-slavery and pro-Secessionist groups and families of the northern Missouri counties promptly washed their hands of the whole situation, and the most ardent of these chose to take up residence within the Confederacy. Many pathetic or humorous accounts of the hegira which ensued have since became a portion of Americana. The "Sixty-three-ers" and "Sixty-four-ers" of Missouri legendry have almost as firm a hold on our traditional affection as the Forty-niners. Rich slave-holding families sold out—in most cases, to remarkable advantage, since there were many bidders for every inch of property. They moved to Kentucky, Tennessee and Arkansas, to be received with open arms by their late comrades. A former Confederate general, Sterling Price, eventually became a Confederate senator from Tennessee.

The retention of Missouri in the Union was regarded as an event of signal importance in the West, and as a matter especially vital to her closest neighbors—Kansas, Nebraska, Iowa and Illinois. Attention in the East, however, was focused upon the future status of West Virginia, the struggle for the eastern shore of Maryland, and the problem of Washington, D.C.

In Richmond, Virginia's more vociferous patriots demanded immediate re-acquisition of those counties of northwestern Virginia which had formed a new State and so recently attached themselves to the United States (formal admission: June 19th, 1863). Following the piecemeal destruction of the Army of the Potomac, Confederate commanders of troops in the Harpers Ferry region and farther up the

Valley of Virginia had, on their own responsibility, thrown out columns through mountains to the west. (In one case at least there was out-and-out expression of intent to seize and subjugate the city of Charleston.) The advancing Secessionists were halted with heavy losses, inflicted by Federal troops still holding the region, together with West Virginia militia and hastily armed parties of enraged citizens. Governor Arthur I. Boreman issued a manifesto in which he declared that the mother state, Virginia, stood guilty of abrogating morally the doctrine of Secession which had now achieved a dignity of historical stature. Quoting the *lives, fortunes and sacred honor* phrase of the original Declaration of Independence, Governor Boreman flung back in the teeth of the Secessionists their own statements, uttered devoutly in earlier years.

"We West Virginians stand as intentioned spiritually as we do physically," he declared, "to uphold the doctrine of self-determination as staunchly as any Virginian, living or dead, ever upheld it against the fancied domination of the North." *Save West Virginia!* became a rallying cry throughout southeastern Ohio and south-western Pennsylvania. Within three days after the publication of this firm stand, Federal artillery brigades were wheeling into position in the mountains.

In Richmond ex-President Lincoln was reputed to have pleaded personally with Jefferson Davis to avoid further bloodshed. Lamon, in his memoirs,* hints that a meeting came about, but gives few details. Whether he was impressed by Boreman's plea or not, or whether he was considerate merely of the practical military problems involved (obviously these were tremendous, because of the nature of the terrain) Davis soon persuaded his impetuous commanders not to proceed further on what might have turned out to be an exceedingly ill-starred campaign. The admission of West Virginia to the Union was acknowledged by the Southern Confederacy, and was included as an integral part of the Washington Treaty signed on December 16th, 1863.

Recollections of A Cavalier. Ward Hill Lamon. (Philadelphia). J. B. Lippincott Company. 1887.

When the Army of the Potomac was destroyed during the first week of July, Major General Sickles managed to salvage the bulk of Major General David B. Birney's Division of his corps, together with remnants of Brigadier General Andrew A. Humphreys' Division. In a rapid retreat across northern Maryland, Sickles was joined also by most of the "Philadelphia Brigade" and a few other regiments of Brigadier General John Gibbon's Division, Second Corps. Lee was occupied with erasing the Union Fifth and Sixth Corps from the landscape, so Sickles had been harried during his march only by small detachments of Confederate cavalry who soon turned back to rejoin Stuart.

Sickles explained afterward that he knew a retreat in a southerly direction would be fatal. In the absence of specific orders from Meade, he decided to take up a defensive position on the left bank of the Susquehanna. There he might resist any approach of the enemy aimed at Wilmington and Philadelphia. (Meade did indeed send him orders to the contrary, by three couriers, but all of those messengers were killed or captured before they could reach Sickles.)

Whatever the motive of the Third Corps commander, his movement served one grain of useful purpose. It affirmed the retention of Cecil County, Maryland, by the Union. Sickles desired mightily to take over the entire eastern shore of that State. . . . He would have needed Napoleon's entire army and Drake's entire navy to occupy the region successfully: pro-Southern sentiment had always run high on the Del-Mar-Va peninsula. Chincoteague Island, Virginia, voted against Secession at the outbreak of the war, but by a narrow margin. Many residents of Delaware, a loyal State (although a slave State), went south to join the Confederates.

Sickles' occupation of Cecil County kept that one small area of Maryland in the Union. Snuggled as they were against Pennsylvania and northern Delaware, the residents boasted a preponderance of pro-Federal belief. This county was later attached to the dismembered State of Delaware, after Sussex County had registered a top-heavy sentiment for leaving its parent Commonwealth and joining adjacent Maryland in cleaving to the Confederate States of America.

By autumn a new frontier was established, for all practical purposes, and was later affirmed by signatories of the Washington Treaty.

The North had lost all of Maryland except Cecil County of that State, and had lost also the southernmost county of Delaware. The North had lost the State of Kentucky. The North had gained the new State of West Virginia, with at least the reluctant blessing of the peace conference. Missouri also was retained. Kansas was not even mentioned in the treaty: this region of one-time bloody contention had been admitted to the Union more than two months before the firing on Fort Sumter, and was occupied by ardent Free-Soilers.

And the North lost Washington, D.C.

Actually this blow to national prestige was delivered not by any cogitation of diplomats, but by the mere fact of Washington's geographical location: it was ordained historically in the moment of Maryland's official espousal of the Confederacy. Obviously the capital of a country could not exist or function if planted within the boundaries of a rival nation.

In a manner of symbolism, however, it was the most bitter potion which the North was compelled to swallow in the awful dosage of defeat. The core, the brain, the heart center, nerve center of the United States of America, necessarily handed over to the Confederate States of America—complete with its Government buildings, its new Capitol, its storied White House, the monuments and traditions and memories—! Veterans of Bull Run and Antietam looked at one another with stony gaze; curses crept from their lips. Loyal women cried, loyal deacons prayed, children wailed questions which were beyond answering. The taunts of a hostile foreign press sounded from abroad.

Washington had to go, there was no help for it. Resumption of a disheartening conflict, stemming solely from a desire to keep Maryland in the Union, was the only alternative. Despite the fury of anguished patriots, and fevered accusations of *Betrayal!* hurled at peace delegates from the North, the District of Columbia was handed over to the Confederacy (it was promptly renamed the District of Dixie).

Less misery attended a compromise relating to disposition of the Indian Territory, although the peacemakers struggled for nearly a month with this question alone. That barren region lay very nearly surrounded on three sides by Confederate states; yet Northern delegates resisted strenuously all persuasions to award the area to the South. At last, urgency demanded that the problem be placed in abeyance; this was done by the establishment of a joint commission for future arbitration. All forts within the Territory were ordered to be vacated (an act condemned by trans-Mississippi congressmen, and one which engendered almost endless disputes and hazards).

At noon on the 16th of December, ink was drying on the treaty's signatures. Noted names were affixed: such as Stephens, Semmes and Johnston for the South . . . Seward, Greeley and McClellan for the North . . . commissioners selected by their respective governments in Richmond and Philadelphia.

Thirteen Southern States, a compact Confederacy.

And now only twenty-two Northern States. California and Oregon were separated from the rest by vast territorial regions with dignity of Statehood to be achieved in the future.

By request of the Confederates, the language of the original Declaration was reemployed in affirming "that these [States] are and of right ought to be, free and independent." There was some haggling on the subject of reparations, then the matter was put aside; it was revived sporadically later in both Congresses, but eventually came by way of being an international jest. (Washington City, most folks felt had been reparation enough.) On the whole, the commissioners worked with laudable despatch; and so, to the amazement of the world, did both Congresses and Executives when it came to ratification. The Confederate States ratified the treaty on Monday, December 28th; the United States two days later.

Perforce the Southern offices would remain in Richmond until the United States had removed its own baggage from Washington—a huge physical encumbrance of two generations' legislative and executive and judicial accumulation. June 1st, 1864, was set as the date of formal withdrawal; the United States to pay all costs of labor and transportation; and it was agreed that Confederate troops should perform guard duty throughout the operation below the new international boundary (the commissioners recognized complications if Northern troops were to operate in such capacity.)

Philadelphia, an emergency capital during the previous summer, would continue to serve as temporary capital. But the proponents of a plan for the designation of Philadelphia as the permanent site met with a storm of objection from every State west of the Alleghenies. Even President Hamlin, a Maine man, promised that he would veto any plan for the establishment of a new capital on the Atlantic seaboard. Congress rocked with debate, week after week; the newspapers fulminated, sneered, grew sage in advice. There were plans for carving a model city out of fresh wilderness, as Washington City had been carved originally. But the physical disadvantages of that plan were apparent.

Freshly built wooden warehouses which stretched their dreary length along the outskirts of Philadelphia filled more solidly with impedimenta of the Government, week after week. Night and day the long trains rumbled up through Maryland with their precious freight of files, furniture, records, statuary, relics, portraits, documents. The housing situation was deplorable; a "model" city of temporary barracks was set up on the banks of the Schuylkill River for the benefit of unhappy Government employees and their families. At times there appeared to be, as Artemus Ward wrote, "a lot more kayose in the Pees then in the War."

America sighed with relief when, in March of 1864, after months of wrangling, the new site was selected. It was Columbus, Ohio. With the approval of voters offered at a special election, the State of Ohio removed its own capital to Cleveland, and ceded a 100-square-mile district to the Nation. In this area the name of the District of Columbia was perpetuated; the city itself was renamed Columbia. Blasting, hammering—the marble-cutting, the straining of hoists began. Through the 1860s armies of workmen toiled and a mat of dust lay thick above the confluence of two Ohio rivers. Slowly the new capital took shape.

(Three successive bond issues were authorized, to pay for it. But these were not sufficient; heavier taxation was the final result, and many tax increases were not repealed for years to come. Secretary of State William H. Seward was compelled to give up his dream of purchasing Russian America. "Seward's Folly" was openly laughed about in Congress, and no political machination could ever bring the matter to a vote. Seward, who served again as Secretary of State during Hamlin's second term, insisted to his dying day that he was right and that the purchase should have been made. But public opinion appeared to have crystalized in the assertion of the irrepressible Artemus Ward: "I kind of gess that what we need is a noo Kapital insted of an iceburg.")

Monday night, July 4th, 1864, the Confederacy celebrated President Davis's arrival at the White House in Washington with a fabulous reception and ball. This event assumed a social and political importance unrivaled in Southern history. Fifty years afterward, if an elderly woman whispered, "I was at The Ball," everyone understood the reference; and the proudest boast of any aging poverty-stricken one-time politician was assuredly the same.

A few Northern dignitaries were invited to attend. Almost to a man the civilians declined, with the exception of the peace commissioners of the previous winter, who felt that their presence might have a salubrious effect upon rela-

tions between the two countries. Some of the military did accept, but they paid their respects with restraint, and most of them retired from the scene at an early hour. Dancers whirled in waltzes in the East Room and the parlors; old portraits of Washington and new (posthumous) portraits of Stonewall Jackson and Albert Sidney Johnston looked down solemnly on the revelers. As well as the original Fourth of July, the first anniversary of the victories at Vicksburg and Gettysburg was being observed officially.

The red-bearded J. E. B. Stuart, proud of his new lieutenant-general's commission, prouder still of the charming wife with whom he jounced in a polka, found time to establish himself before a throng of admirers and recite one of his characteristic flights into poesy:

"When Mars with his stentorian blare
Decreed that spears of war must fly,
He little recked that cannons' glare
Would paint the chill of Northern sky!
The Dove of Peace now perches cool,
And Venus offers balm to all—"

No longer was there an auburn-haired Kate Chase wielding the imperious wand of her beauty, no longer was there a Mary Todd Lincoln to set tongues gossiping by the extravagance of her gowns. Mrs. Kate Chase Sprague was now circulating a little less imperiously in dull, crowded Philadelphia. And Mary Todd Lincoln was in Illinois.

So was her husband, the only President of the United States to resign his office. Released from detention in Richmond a month before (as a pronounced gesture of international amity) he had withdrawn quietly to his former home at Springfield.

There patiently he endured the flood of calumny, vituperation and mere criticism which rushed around him; there he received the rare affirmation of personal loyalty and affection from friends who still clung; and from there he went, a few months afterward, to practice law in Chicago, along with the stout Lamon.

More profitable legal business than he might have believed possible came Mr. Lincoln's way. "Hill," he said to his worshiping partner in March, "I thought to be turned out to grass, and winter-killed grass at that. Never did I expect to discover a downright clover patch!" On the evening of April 14th, 1865, he went to McVicker's Theatre where Taylor's trivial play, *Our American Cousin,* was being presented. There, while seated with friends in a box, he was shot to death by an actor whose hatred for Abraham Lincoln had survived all changes of status and of capitals, all affirmations of Peace.

The honeymoon of war was ended. The Confederacy was now faced with the inexorable necessity for an adjustment to those mundane housekeeping tasks which a nation must accomplish, daily and yearly and eternally, if it is to dwell with itself in domestic harmony and productivity. The Southern States, by act of conflict, had annulled a distasteful marriage to the original Federal Government. But the establishment of their national independence had in no way resolved the cumulative problems of individual commonwealths' cooperation within a centralized structure."

Thus cogently has the basic perplexity of

the new Confederate States of America been summed up by an astute political observer and historian.*

The same situation might not exist in peace which had prevailed when the Confederacy was animated by the grim demands and pressures of warfare . . . even then the Nation had fumbled severely. Cabinet member after cabinet member was appointed and confirmed, only to offer an early resignation. The interference of Mr. Davis with his generals had been typified as a scandal by outspoken critics of his administration, and men of as exalted position as Robert Toombs had been placed under arrest. The frail but thorny Vice-President, Alexander Stephens, openly affirmed his disapproval of many of Mr. Davis's policies. A young Confederate officer in Texas stated in public that he should like to run his sword through the heart of Sam Houston; and only a few years previously Houston had been idolized as the savior of the Lone Star State. A grumble of "too much Virginia" was

---

*Western Experiments in Republican Formation. Dame Rosemary Tommey. London. Longmans, Green and Company. 1905.

current throughout the armies, and angry North Carolinians insisted that they were robbed of military opportunity and credit. Yet the war had been fought by the South to a successful conclusion. The dissident States achieved independence, but, in the opinion of much of the outside world, did not know what to do with it. Angry bickering between the States, and opinionated resistance to the authority of Washington, characterized the rest of Davis's administration. Only when President Robert E. Lee entered the White House, in 1868, did rivalries go into temporary abeyance, and the momentary lessening of dispute may be ascribed almost as much to the so-called "Veterans' Reform Congress," as to any other cause.

The government under Lee achieved a measure of serenity; but this seemed merely a duplication and protraction of wartime illusion. Basic problems and conflicts had not been solved: they had only been put aside for a time. And it was no extraneous power which worked toward confusion of the new nation: congenitally Dixie carried the seeds of internal sickness within its own loins. Open identification of these ills was like a reversion to the slogans and

phrases of wartime. They were two: States' rights, and slavery. They were cured almost simultaneously.

There existed noticeable jealousy between the extreme trans-Mississippi region and the bulk of the Confederacy. In attitude Texas stood aloof from her neighbors, Louisiana and Arkansas. In history, population and ambition, Texas was dissimilar. The fire of that original independence which had been established for more than five years, only a young lifetime in the past, could not be put down; nor, amid ardent Texans, was there much desire to extinguish it. Beyond the Sabine River dwelt many vociferous ex-soldiers who asserted that they had but exchanged one brand of Washingtonian tyranny for another. Even during the beneficent Lee administration there were two occasions when Texas senators and representatives stalked from the legislative chambers in dudgeon, to return only after a process of cajolery and mediation was indulged in.

The great State had entered a period of almost immediate internal prosperity, as its cattle herds began to swell in multitude, and as a hungry United States clamored for beef. There might be at the time no economical transportation of beef, either slaughtered or on the hoof, from Texas to her sister States at the East. But cattle could be driven cheaply across the dusty neglected Indian Territory, and into corrals springing up alongside new Kansas railroads. Furthermore, the general table economy of the South was adjusted on a self-sustaining basis, region by region. There was not the taste or market for beef which Texans found in the North. Other Southern commonwealths might envy the flow of Yankee gold into Texas; they could not duplicate it, even in cotton and tobacco. Prosperity from these sources was a thing to be achieved in slower and more cumulative fashion.

Texans recognized a sore point in the fact that combined deliberations of years had brought no answer to the Indian Territory question. The commissioners who juggled this international-continental hot potato were continually being replaced; they'd had their political fingers scorched in the process. And, North and South alike, the acceptance of appointment to the joint Indian Territorial Commission began to be regarded as residence in a political graveyard. Four different compromise treaties were tendered for ratification before 1875; two had been rejected by the Confederacy, two by the United States.

On March 2nd, 1878, a column of some fifteen hundred Texans, who had been trained and armed in secrecy, rode north across the Red River, and deployed at strategic points throughout the Indian Territory. There were no garrisons of either Confederate or United States troops in the region: such strongpoints had been expressly forbidden by the Washington Treaty of 1863, and only a few white traders or outlaws were resident. Rumors about the intended *coup d'état* had of course reached both Washington and Columbia, but generally were discounted by those in authority.

In the most embittered language which had been employed diplomatically since the war, Columbia demanded that Washington order the immediate withdrawal of Texas troops. To the Union's satisfaction, President John B. Gordon of the Confederacy resisted sternly the advice of those militants who urged that Confederate army forces should be sent to support the Texans.

"Do the gentlemen desire a renewal of fratricidal strife on this continent?" Gordon returned witheringly. "Would the gentlemen ordain a Manassas and a Chancellorsville in the unpopulated sagebrush country?" Empowered by a hastily-summoned Congress, President Gordon forthwith directed that Governor Houston Lockey of Texas remove his "militia" from the disputed area. This Lockey refused to do. He said that they were not State militia as such—they were private individuals, and that his authority over them did not extend beyond Texas boundaries.

In the North, Abolitionists of the old days raised their voices, crying that United States territory had been invaded, and that troops were needed immediately to expel the Texans. The most reactionary press exclaimed that once more North and South stood on the brink of war; but public apathy was at first astounding, and, later, quite understandable. This was the fruit of fifteen years of haggling by the joint commission. The Indian Territory problem was too old, too shop-worn, it seemed no part of the angry present.

At an unprecedented rate, Northern migration had been flowing into the West. A steel fabric of railroads was knitting the Pacific States ever more tightly into the Union. Despite Indian resistance in the northwest and southwest, hordes of settlers had pushed their way into previously untenanted wastes. Reiterating the Young-Man-Go-West counsel which he had given Josiah B. Grinnell in a previous generation, Horace Greeley declared in 1872: "It is a phenomenon unparalleled, a pageant previously unwitnessed. Perhaps a third of a million Americans in the prime of manhood are now striding in their haleness, who might be devoid of breath and heartbeat had the War of the Southern Revolution been prolonged.... They must move somewhere. Let them move to the West."

By-passing the unattractive riddle of the Indian Territory, a sweep of westward settlement had filled Kansas, Nebraska and Colorado— oozing indelibly up toward Oregon and the Washington Territory, seeping down into mineral-rich mountains which extended north of the Mexican border. Citizens of the United States possessed neither the time, energy nor will to take up arms for the retention (many spoke of it as the acquisition) of a region commonly declared to be unproductive and without charm for the land-hungry. Only a handful of fanatical Kansas volunteers galloped south, declaring an intention to banish all Texans from the area. Long-range rifles whirred, there were ambuscades and bushwhacking attended with small loss of life on either side. Governor Lockey made bold to order in the Texas Rangers, and the Kansans were compelled to flee. Both parties, it turned out, had more to fear from Indian attack than from each other.

The Southern Confederacy was compelled to face the unpleasant fact that this constituted the first flouting of the Nation's authority by a single State which had come about (except in the matter of reluctant payment of taxes). The Confederate Secretary of War ordered a disposition of troops along the borders of Louisiana and Arkansas, the Secretary of the Navy sent warships to lie outside Galveston and Corpus Christi. There was now more chance of open warfare between Texas and the Confederacy than between the Confederacy and the North. But the brigades did not move, and thousands of wary Texans stood ready to dispute their passage into the State . . . cannon were being moved

into position to defend the harbors.

When, on April 21st (the anniversary of the Battle of San Jacinto) a wildly enthusiastic legislature at Austin declared for secession from the Confederacy, and when, two days later, Houston Lockey was named as provisional President of the second Republic of Texas, not a shot was exchanged between opposing forces along the State's margins.

Nor did the United States draw its sword. A perplexing no-man's-land of baked plains and rough hillocks stood assimilated by Texas. The Indian Territory problem no longer existed, and the Northern public appeared glad to be rid of it.

A basic doctrine of self-determination by a commonwealth had been reasserted and redemonstrated, to the Confederacy's vexation. But the loss of Texas redounded to the eventual advantage of the Southern nation, since the need for a strong centralized authority of government had become sadly apparent; and from that time forth the political tide flowed toward delocalization of sovereignty.

"I am not, nor ever have been, in favor of bringing about in any way the social and political equality of the white and black races."

"There must be the position of the superiors and the inferiors; and . . . I, as much as any other man, am in favor of the superior position being assigned to the white man."

These were not the utterances of a Toombs or a Stephens or a Barksdale, and the words were spoken not south of the Ohio River but north of it. They were spoken by Abraham Lincoln at Charleston, Illinois, in September, 1858. They were not exactly a defense of human slavery, but neither did they intimate that Lincoln would ever promulgate an Emancipation Proclamation. Seasons and circumstances may alter original attitudes.

Dolorously the Confederate States of America heard and felt the mutterings of abolition within their own bulk. It was the trend of the nineteenth century and could no longer be ignored or denied. Equally it was impossible in the Republic of Texas (although slaves proportionately were fewer there) for men to escape eternally from an humanitarian obligation.

Such a nation as Argentina, laboring supposedly under an archaic system, had decreed that all children born to slaves after January 31st, 1813, should be free. Mexico freed her slaves in 1829. Officially there were no slaves in British colonies after 1838, nor in French colonies after 1848. Texas and the Confederate States labored under the weight of an institution as unsound economically as it was repugnant spiritually.

Defenders of a designated Holy system—those who invoked Biblical texts to support their tenet—were dying out. New voices were heard, and some of them rose from surprising sources. The Jeffersonian party was a force to be reckoned with. It had been founded in the certainty that liberation must come about; and was named for the revered statesman who had, long before, manumitted his own slaves. So had Robert E. Lee, so had hosts of other eminent Confederates. . . .

Admired officials such as Stephen Dodson Ramseur (he owned a brilliant record during the war of 1861–63, and became Confederate Secretary of War in 1880) lent their strength to the Jeffersonians. Emotionally and intellectually the Confederacy could not with blandness ignore the belief and example of those very men who had been most instrumental in securing the prized independence. A former chief-of-staff of the army, General Robert E. Rodes, made bold to sit upon a platform with State chairmen of the Jeffersonian party, shortly after he resigned his commission in 1878. (Rodes wished to put down the Texas rebellion by force of arms, and was chagrined at the failure of his Government to act.) Even General John Pegram, who succeeded Rodes in command, was alleged to embrace the same principles.

The Dutch began a liberation policy in 1863, the United States of America ratified the thirteenth amendment late in 1865. Spain, in 1870, had decreed the freedom of all slaves reaching the age of sixty years, and made provision for the gradual emancipation of younger ones. Even Brazil adopted a twenty-one-year clause in 1871, which eventually would bring freedom to all.

The Southern republics of North America sat alone, clinging uncertainly to a system no longer justified by plutology or in the philosophy of their enlightened citizens.

Various States had acted independently. Virginia and Kentucky went "Free" during the last year of the Lee administration; North Carolina joined them in 1876. In Texas there had been a vigorous attempt to insert a liberation clause in the constitution of the Republic, though this was voted down.

"A Divine light may be seen at times," wrote a venerable bishop and former Confederate lieutenant general, as he assembled the impressions received during his busy life.* "It reveals the errors of humanity as assuredly it illuminates the pathway toward which a traveler must turn if he is to avoid any duplication of the same ambuscades. Both Honor and Devotion demand the acceptance of a route which, though it may lead temporarily amid wastes of humiliating regret and mortification, is the unprofaned highway toward a repentant Future."

The implication in this statement is that the South had a choice. Actually it had none. Progressive enlightenment and reform among the

---

*A Tale That Is Told. Leonidas Polk. (New Orleans). Bandel, Linn and Company. 1884.

nations at large had deleted any excuse for a protraction of human slavery. No longer might the question be, *What?* but only *When?* and *How?* Sullen or hysterical resistance by stubborn cliques in the various States could but accelerate an exertion of power by the central government. When Maryland and Tennessee declared for liberation (by the 1880s, freed blacks in the Confederacy nearly equaled the slave population) the Jeffersonians received multitudes of fresh converts from younger and more liberal elements in other States as well.

Now there was little resistance worthy of the name. The Liberation Act (with provision for financial restitution of slaveowners) passed both houses of Congress early in 1885 by a comfortable margin, as did an accompanying constitutional amendment. Ratification of the latter was accomplished speedily by every State. Remarkable transportational and mechanical developments of the previous decade played their part in the decision, most certainly; but a long view of ethical and moral principles had its salubrious effect throughout the population.

People of the new Republic of Texas duplicated their neighbors' resolution only four months later.

"We stand fortunate," said President James Longstreet, in a message to the Nation on Freedom Day (April 13th, 1885), "in that this reform has been accomplished by self-determination, and not by the infliction of a discipline which could and should have been resented. We must award increasing reverence to the memory of martyrs who died to achieve our independence. Had we, the Confederate States of America, gone down in defeat, there might have ensued a period of enforced amalgamation replete with every imaginable domestic horror. A common hatred directed against the Negro, which we do not now demonstrate or even possess, would have been the inevitable result."

President Longstreet went on to point out the high degree of literacy and skills already demonstrated by the blacks, and to praise the efforts of citizens who had established the Freedmen's Agricultural and Mechanical Schools.

"Public funds shall be employed to extend such benefits to all. I foresee a time when even the aptitude for suffrage may be gained by those emancipated. Let us welcome these faithful people into our economic structure, and profit mutually through them and with them. Let us give thanks to Almighty God that this great good was achieved in accord with a changing time, and in harmonious acceptance by all. I believe that a fevered dislocation of our entire system would have but substituted brutality for human courtesy, suspicion for common trust, and would have engendered a fundamental antagonism."

Many of the best minds, both in the United and in the Confederate States, were keenly aware of benefits accruing twenty-two years previously by the cessation of a fratricidal war within twenty-eight months after its beginning. This opinion was reaffirmed constantly by spokesmen, North and South, throughout the decades. It grew to be an international attitude; and eventually was reiterated even by fundamentalists at the North, who insisted originally that the tragedies of Gettysburg and Vicksburg dealt the United States of America a blow fully mortal.

No less a personage than James Birdseye McPherson, nineteenth President of the United States, referred to this fact in his second inaugural address, which is now familiar to most schoolboys.

"Both we and our respected neighbors at the South," said President McPherson, "must look upon the separation which ensued as a matter transcending national boundaries but of deepest concern to our combined American spirit. The Confederate States were indeed victorious, and the doctrine of Federal resistance to a choice of secession was disproved. But the human heart, and the American human happiness, achieved a victory far more extensive. Had the hideous attrition of the campaigns in 1862 and 1863 been extended—or perhaps even intensified—for another two years, the vigor of the young population upon our Continent might have been bled into whiteness. Vast populations, now living heartily and productively, might be mere relic bones in Virginia loam or in Georgia clay. We must turn toward the Past without recrimination, and, by the same token, face our Future with that thankfulness which is born only of high courage. We must reach

across that boundary which is no longer forti-
fied, no longer the sentry-beat of armed men.
We must embrace those patriots of the South,
no longer to be typified as dissident and rebel-
lious, and with them declare: 'Give thanks to
God that it ended when it did! Better two alert
nations, still strong in the muscle and spirit of
youth, than one confused and weakened entity
dyed deeply with the sentiment of sectionalism,
and befouled by angry wounds which might not
heal for a century to follow!' "

President McPherson's expressed opinions
drew immediate and favorable response from
Confederate leaders. The colorful Southern Senator and former cavalry chief, Jeb Stuart, for
example, applauded the Northern Executive's
sentiments by telegraph, by personal letter
which followed, and by a speech in the Confederate Senate at Washington only a week later.
A. P. Hill, at the time Confederate Secretary of
War, also concurred, although perhaps less
flamboyantly, President McPherson's utterance
had met with some lack of acceptance by certain segments of the Northern press; but was
greeted with enthusiasm by Confederate editors.

Still, it was not Senator Stuart himself, but his son, R. E. L. Stuart—the Rel Stuart of dashing Spanish war fame, hero of the brief Confederate campaign waged in Cuba in 1898—who became eventually a vital and articulate proponent of those principles peculiar to the Consolidation parties. (These appeared in the three nations during early years of the twentieth century.) Consolidationists found their most effective leadership (in the Confederacy, at least) in the person of that great Virginian, Woodrow Wilson, eleventh President of the Confederate States of America.

Rel Stuart, born in 1867, had all of his father's intrepidity and assertiveness. These qualities, which some people found distasteful in the picturesque sire, were disciplined in the case of the son by application of a calm and tolerant restraint. Rel Stuart did not join in the numerous filibustering expeditions to Cuba which became the plaything of young Confederates and Texans during the 1880s and 1890s. Stuart, although trained for a military career, resigned from the C.S. Army at the age of twenty-nine to go to Congress. There he distinguished himself quickly by displaying perceptive quali-

ties of leadership. When the battleship *Mississippi* was blown up and sunk, in Havana harbor
on the night of February 15th, 1898, Robert E.
Lee Stuart affirmed (along with the rest of the
Congress) that a state of war existed and should
exist between the kingdom of Spain and the
Confederate States.

Within forty-eight hours following the decisive action at Washington he had resigned as
Representative, and accepted a commission,
taking immediate command of a brigade under
General Fitzhugh Lee, who was to head the ex-
peditionary force. Soon in command of a division, Rel Stuart, in a lightning campaign, swept
through Cuba and nullified Spanish resistance.
It was regarded as the decisive land operation
of that brief but violent war. It was not unex-
pected that he should come to be known (following the treaty of peace signed on December
10th, 1898) as "The Modern Father of Cuban
Annexation." Fervently interested in the rehabil-
itation of the Cuban people, and in the re-
building of cities and plantations destroyed by
warfare, Stuart served successively as Military
Governor of the occupied island, provisional
Governor of the Territory, following its estab-

lishment; and for two terms as Governor of the State of Cuba, after its admission into the Confederacy. He is credited, also, with having been a major force in the establishment of Cuba's eventual wealth as sugar capital of the world, rising from an influx of both Confederate States' and United States' money. He was considered to be the author of economic concessions which attracted a flow of funds from New York and New England, so necessary to profitable development of the sugar industry.

In his elder years, while serving as Ambassador to the United States, the internationally admired Rel Stuart often referred humorously to the fact that his life might not have been lived had the war of the 1860s been extended. "Any old campaigner knows," he is reported as having said at a Gridiron Dinner in Columbia in 1930, "that a man in the field can thrust out his neck only about so long, and then the axe of Fate will fall against it. My late father, bless him, was not noted for any reluctance to personally engage the enemy. Suppose one of your Yankee grandfathers had managed to reach him with a pistol bullet, during some minor encounter in Virginia—let us say, at a hamlet like Appomattox Court, Gum Spring, or Yellow Tavern! Why, I should never have been born!—and the great United States of America should have had to worry along without the cooperative services of a brilliant Confederate Ambassador such as myself!"

Stuart was well-loved throughout the American nations, having served as a diplomatic representative to the Republic of Texas, prior to his ambassadorship to the United States. The entire continent was plunged into mourning in 1931, when Rel Stuart—vigorous, active and influential in his sixty-fifth year—died in an airliner crash in Kansas. It was the same catastrophe which claimed the life of Knute Roekne, famous Notre Dame football coach.

The six and one-half decades of Rel Stuart's life were marked by the posing of, and by the complicated ascendancy of, a distinct problem—one to which the twenty-nine years following his death have brought no equable solution. It was the problem of the Negro, and the extent to which a free colored population might be assimilated into the country's economic, political and social structures.

President Longstreet (in the message of April, 1885, quoted *ante*) seemed to assume that eventual difficulties would be minimized because emancipation had not been foisted upon a prostrate South in one fell swoop. But his hopes for a smooth and temperate transition could not be realized. Friction was recognizable immediately; it compounded through the years. The color question became, within a generation or two, the most painful disputation within the Nation.

"There are those who think that this issue will not be resolved short of a thousand years hence," wrote a Confederate statesman of our own time.* "Others are convinced that the pressure of world opinion will bring at least political and economic—if not social—equality to the Negro, before the end of this century. In creasingly plagued by controversy lies the uneasy head of our Country! Sagacious moderates are still stanch in their efforts to achieve a fair ad-

---

*Black, White and Tan. Barton K. Lillwell. (Richmond). James Williams: The Walnut Tree Press. 1940.

justment in professional, commercial and indus-
trial enterprise, in rural economics, and in
higher education. But the extremists of both
factions wrap the barbed-wire of fresh entan-
glements along the paths of conciliation."

And the dilemma of the Southern Nation
was not hers alone, but became a mournful
dowry which necessarily she would fetch along
into any future amalgamation of Americans.

Throughout his public life
Woodrow Wilson carried an ambition for unity.
Despite a boyhood spent in Virginia (some biographers have said *because* of it) he became
imbued early with a fierce belief that Americans
could not achieve their true destiny except in
communion. Beyond that, his hopes were for an
extension of democratic ideal throughout the
world, embracing eventually a fruitful future for
all peoples therein.

He was realist enough to observe that such
a widespread Utopian enterprise could not be
brought about in his own lifetime—perhaps not
in many decades to follow. But the hope was

there, and he felt that an initial linking-up of the American nations must and should occur, as a brilliant example of what might be accomplished, inter-continentally, in a later age.

Also he possessed sufficient political sagacity to refrain from public utterances which might be interpreted as too radical, until he was safely ensconced behind the pulpit of the Confederate Presidency in 1910. Then he began to speak; his own Country and others listened to him—at first with incredulity, often with hostility, but always with awareness.

"A steadfast concert for peace can never be maintained except by a partnership of democratic nations."

"It must be a league of honor, a partnership of opinion."

"The principle for which the South fought meant standstill in the midst of change; it was conservative, not creative; it was against drift and destiny; it protected an impossible institution and a belated order of society; it withstood a creative and imperial idea, the

idea of a united people and a single law
of freedom."

Once more the current of history might
have been diverted and whorled, had not an
amendment to the Confederate constitution
made it possible for the President to be ree-
lected for a second term. Wilson served from
1910 until 1922, though barely he eked out a
victory in 1916 (for some hours it was thought
that the open support he received from Consolidationists had been the kiss of death). But
the entry into World War I of the three American nations, which occurred in 1917, gave the
Consolidationists within those countries enormous stimulation.

Within a single week U.S. President Theodore Roosevelt, C.S. President Woodrow Wilson
and President Roy Smith of Texas all asked
their respective Congress for declarations of
war against Germany. The notion of a common
cause against an enemy was, surprisingly, more
than acceptable to the publics involved; and
when Texas, Confederate and United States
troops were brigaded together overseas, an in-

ternational sentimental approval became immediately discernible.

It should not be necessary at this date to do more than allude to the events of the generation which followed; they are fresh in the minds of all, resplendent with warmth and detail. International trade reached a new peak on the American continent. The last of the protective tariffs fell by the wayside. Texas oil and piped gas poured readily into the United States; tobacco and sugar and textiles of the Confederacy were distributed as acceptably as were automobiles and minerals and cereals of the North. Hollywood films danced on screens in Tampa and Nashville. Consolidationist groups sprouted on every college campus. Yankee vacationists disported themselves in Havana and Florida and New Orleans; booted Texans were an ordinary sight on New York streets.

World War II only affirmed the speedy cohesion of Americans who breathed an identical atmosphere, were rooted to indigenous soil, laved by native rivers. Soldiers, sailors and airmen of all three countries—and black and white and red and brown, as well—assaulted the same beachheads, rolled in the same fleets,

flew on the same missions. The words of the departed Wilson were quoted again, and found welcome in many hearts.

"The South fought for a principle, as the North did; it was this which gave the war dignity, and supplied the tragedy with a double motive."

"Only free peoples can hold their purpose and their honor steady to a common end, and prefer the interests of mankind to any narrow interest of their own."

". . . A universal dominion of right by such a concert of free peoples as shall bring peace and safety to all nations and make the world itself at last free."

A sensitive pundit and philosopher of our own time has summed the situation which prevailed at the end of the war:*

"Exuberance deriving from a heritage more

*The American Ambition. William Dogg. (New York and Cleveland). The World Publishing Company, 1955.

universal than their fathers would admit—
Necessity deriving from an economy more in-
terdependent than their fathers could employ—
Mutual recognition of an earth moistened by
their blood in a commingling, not on opposite
sides of the barricade, but in front of the same
guns—These are components which must bring
the citizens of three Countries into a re-welding,
if there is any such thing as historic justice or
historic verity."

The last bombs of World War II had scarcely ceased their detonation when a march of the
Soviets began to shake the world's freedom.
Somber threat of Communist domination spread
like a cold fog across the oceans, and chilled
the hearts of North Americans, even while they
toiled—but separately, still—to build an ade-
quate defense. Beyond British Columbian mountains lay the colossal menace of Russian America: there airstrips were being extended, there
missile bases were gouged . . . tank brigades deployed on maneuvers. Confederates congratu-
lated themselves on Cuban Annexation—still
fresh in the minds of many living men—but
Texans looked with disquietude across the Rio

Grande into an unpredictable Mexico; and all three Nations felt uncertain tremors in every wind which came from the northwest.

It was in this time that seed sown by the Wilsons and Stuarts of the past could germinate. A persuasive heat of common peril, the rains of angry determination, brought the plant into flower.

By quiet agreement of the Consolidationists in those three countries, long-promised and long-contemplated legislation was introduced simultaneously at Columbia, Washington and Austin, late in 1959. The way of parliamentarians became difficult for the few months ensuing; but action was accelerated during the next sessions of the Congresses. By midsummer Consolidationists began to scent a victory.

But the year of 1960 had nearly run its course before—by dint of judicial deliberation, legislative endeavor and executive approval—the two younger Nations were ready to join with the United States in fateful conclave—to set up machinery for that reassembling of American power which had become an almost religious necessity.

In the earnest words of C. S. President

Ambrose Powell Hill (namesake and great-grandson of the Confederate corps commander and Secretary of War): "Our three countries must not only make common cause in the present world crisis, but must abide by a common law and be inspired by the original American dream. If we have lost a century of mutual endeavor we shall rectify that loss by a devotion more concentrated, and an effulgence unique in the annals of mankind."

This week, in Washington, District of Dixie, in the Confederate States of America, President Hill and the President of the United States and the President of Texas will join, with their respective Secretaries of State, in deliberations for the purpose of effecting a reunion and integration of the American peoples.

Unanimously, and with obvious approval of the several publics, Washington was selected because of its general historical associations unshared by Columbia and Austin.

Official opening of the conference will occur on Wednesday evening, April 12th. This date marks the centennial of the firing on Fort Sumter.

The initial session, including only an invocation to be followed with brief addresses by the three Presidents, will be televised internationally at nine P.M., Eastern Standard Time.

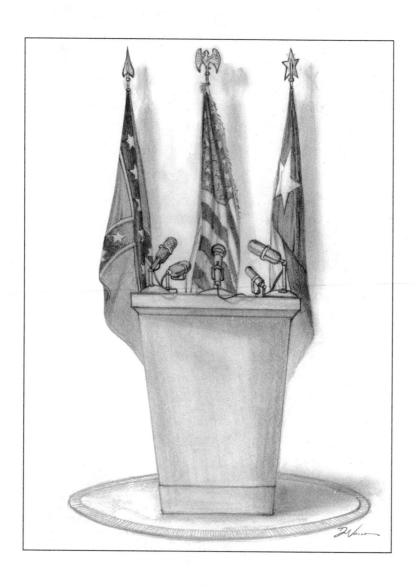

AN HISTORICAL INVERSION

In June, 1959, Irene and I were living in the old Noel Coward house—Goldenhurst—which we had taken for the summer and early autumn. That's in England, in Kent near the village of Aldington. One day I received a letter from (the late) Daniel Mich, then executive editor of *Look* magazine. He was flying over from the U.S. to London, and wanted me to meet him there. "Something very important to discuss," etc., etc.

He telephoned me from his hotel a few days later. I told him that there was no point in my coming up to London. I was deeply immersed in *Spirit Lake,* and would be for a couple of years to come. He said that didn't matter, and to please come anyway and talk; he said that he could tell me everything necessary in an hour or so.

So I took the train up from Ashford in the morning, and had lunch with Mich and his wife in their suite at Claridge's. When he told me what he and Mike Cowles wanted me to do, I shook my head.

What would it have been like if the South had won the Civil War?

I was far away from the Civil War path, and had been for years, and owned no desire to resume treading that thorny sentry-beat.

The handsome white-haired Dan looked at me quizzically.

"You know, I hear things about you. I hear that you never take a vacation."

"Right," said I. "I can't. If I try, I go nuts. I just can't relax without some work to do. The few times I've tried to take a vacation, all I did was to drink solidly for a couple of weeks or months, and that's no good."

He asked, "What are you doing over here in England?"

"Studying up on Kent. There are some Kentish characters in *Spirit Lake*. But it's a good change, you see, to go to another country when I'm working on an enormous and difficult book. Somehow there's stimulation in going into a new environment."

Mich said, "Tell me this: Have you ever thought of just changing your work, instead of changing your location?" He went on to explain in detail what he meant. In other words, after this long grind with *Spirit Lake* he was contending that it might do me good, and offer a stimulus, if I worked for a time on material utterly unrelated to the larger task at hand.

I thought this over for a while, and although I wasn't beguiled into believing that Dan's whole purpose in having me meet him in London was altruistic, nevertheless I thought there might be some grains of truth there.

"I'd like to know what my editor-agent thinks about this."

"Well," he said, "why don't you find out

right now? Let's see—it's two or three o'clock here—" (whatever it was)—"Do you know where to reach Donald Friede now?"

I called New York and got Donald. I told him what Dan Mich had in mind. Donald said, "I want to think this over, and I want to talk to Bill Targ, and maybe to Jerry Fried. Anyway, I want to talk to *somebody*. What time will you be home?" I told him what time I'd be back in Kent, and he said, "I'll call you this afternoon— or rather this evening, your time."

... I hadn't been back at Goldenhurst twenty minutes when Donald was on the phone. He said that he had talked to his wife, Eleanor, and all concerned at World, and everyone was in unanimous agreement that it would do me good and no harm to stop *Spirit Lake* in some future month long enough to do the *Look* piece. I warned Donald that that might take two or three months, including brushing up on Civil War research, and all. He said he still felt the same way about it, and should he go ahead and make a deal? (Mich was returning to New York in another day or two.) I told him Yes, go ahead: call Mich as soon as the latter arrived in New York, and make a date.

What should he ask?—Donald wondered aloud. I said, "My suggestion is to ask $25,000 for the serial rights, and drop down to $20,000 if necessary." Then I called Mich at Claridge's and got him just as he and his wife were walking to the door to go out for the evening. I told him it was all set: I'd do the job, and Donald would arrange the business end of it after Mich was back in the United States. I also stipulated a deadline not before September, 1960.

Donald called me the next week and said, "That was about the toughest deal I ever made in my life. It took exactly seven minutes from the time I walked into the office." He asked $25,000 for the serial rights only. As I had more or less prophesied, they howled, and came back with a counter-offer of $20,000. Donald accepted that, and walked out. Of course all the subsidiary rights belonged to me.

Early the next winter, returning to New York en route to Sarasota, I had a visit with the *Look* people, and reiterated an original request for autonomy in my delineation of what might have occurred had the South won the Civil War. This was again promised to me.

A guess was made that everybody and his

dog who read that particular issue of *Look*, would have his own personal theories, and that they would be at variance with my own.

I groaned. "They'll all be writing letters."

Dan Mich smiled, and observed, "Isn't that what we want them to do?"

The letters came, all right, as soon as the story was published (it took up the bulk of the November 22nd, 1960, issue). Promptly the public deluged us with mail and telegrams. I recall that one of the latter was from a seventeen-year-old high school boy, who said that he was so indignant he couldn't wait to write a letter—he'd have to spend his hard-earned money on a telegram instead. "Don't you know that Ulysses S. Grant survived the Civil War, and lived to become President of the *United States*? How dare you call yourself an *historian*?"

Of the letters, a couple came from former President Harry S Truman and Upton Sinclair. One of these gentlemen stated and the other implied that he had been reading about the Civil War before I was born. I was inclined to agree in each case. "Yes. But not so *thoroughly*."

Strangely enough, very few fire-eating Rebels objected to my statement in reviewing the imaginary situation at Gettysburg: "Lee's attitude was a marvel to those about him. He was decisive, incisive; and the orders which he issued brooked no misinterpretation." I guess the idea was that this was a flattering presentation, if historically untrue. So the Southerners were content.

In identical fashion there was no resentment manifested when I wrote, in reviewing the situation in Mississippi, that the Union campaign, "so auspiciously begun, might still have been concluded successfully had the Confederate President and his two field commanders, Johnston and Pemberton, descended into contradiction and confusion." Of course that was exactly what the relationship descended into, and it became a contributing factor to the Confederates' loss of Vicksburg.

Once again, this seemed like a cute little falsehood to utter about Jefferson Davis. So the United Daughters of the Confederacy didn't picket my house. Instead they purred whenever we met.

A chronic complaint from other readers was that, in my removal of Grant from the scene thus fortuitously, by accident, I was being just too *expedient.* There wasn't time to answer many of the letters: I had to have a card printed for that purpose. But, had there been time in which to sift out these recurring criticisms, I should have suggested that the correspondents read pages 581 and 582 of the first volume of *Personal Memoirs of U. S. Grant* (New York: Charles L. Webster & Company, 1885).

General Grant speaks of an occurrence in early August, only a little more than a month after the fall of Vicksburg. "During this visit I reviewed Banks' army a short distance above Carrollton. The horse I rode was vicious and but little used, and on my return to New Orleans ran away and, shying at a locomotive in the street, fell, probably on me. I was rendered insensible, and when I regained consciousness I found myself in a hotel near by with several doctors attending me. My leg was swollen from the knee to the thigh, and the swelling, almost to the point of bursting, extended along the body up to the arm-pit. The pain was almost beyond endurance. I lay at the hotel something over a week without being able to turn myself in bed. I had a steamer stop at the nearest point possible, and was carried to it on a litter. I was then taken to Vicksburg, where I remained unable to move for some time afterwards."

Is any further comment necessary on this particular subject?

As a student of Gettysburg, I am convinced that Lee lost the battle because of the ambiguity of his orders and his delegation of choice to Ewell instead of being a determinative commander in his own right. This seemed apparent when I was a very young man, first studying the battle; and nothing discovered since has caused me to change my belief.

O.K. So what would have happened if Lee had suddenly become, as the fictitious British colonel remarks, "a marvel to those about him," and decisive and incisive and all the rest? He would have won the battle much in the way described.

Take it from there. No fight on July 14th at Falling Waters, so Pettigrew would have lived. There would have been no warfare in 1864, and Stuart would have lived, and McPherson. A. P. Hill wouldn't have been shot in the spring of 1865. Those men might have become active in the national or international scene for years to come—just as John B. Gordon, who *did* survive the entire war, was active. Just as Grant, who *did* survive the entire war, was active.

Also may we draw attention to the fact that the quotation attributed to Lincoln (with regard to the social and political equality of the white and black races) is authentic. So is the one which follows, about superiors and inferiors. I didn't invent these observations. Lincoln spoke the words as and when and where related.

The quotations from Woodrow Wilson are true utterances of Wilson's as well.

. . . But I had a ball when it came to my Sittenfields and such. *My Service in Saddle and in Senate* never existed, nor did its author. . . . Houghton Mifflin existed. In 1904? Oh, yes.

The War of the American Secession was never written either, although the Century Company was certainly in business in New York in 1888. . . . We have some fine friends, Kenneth and Reidun Clarke, who actually were our landlord and landlady when we took the Coward house in Kent. So that's where I got *that*.

Take the next one. J. J. Pettigrew was mortally wounded during the Confederate retreat from Gettysburg, so he didn't live to father any H. H. Pettigrew, born in 1870. And John Zacharias, mentioned as the publisher in this case, is in fact another friend: a Greek-American who goes these days by the name of John Z. Clark.

Ward Hill Lamon didn't write any *Recollections of a Cavalier*, published by Lippincott in 1887. And his attempts at a Lincoln biography were muddled and mainly disastrous. . . . *Western Experiments in Republican Formation?* Another invention. Dame Rosemary Tommey didn't ever live. Instead we have our admired English friends, Rosemary and Tommy James.

A Tale That Is Told, by Leonidas Polk, and published in 1884? Nay, nay. That cannon ball was waiting for him on Pine Mountain, down in Georgia, in 1864. But my former crony Bandel Linn is doing well with his programs at a station in Benton Harbor, Michigan—radio or TV, or both, or which? Can't remember.

. . . *Black, White and Tan*, by Barton K. Lillwell. No such book, no such author. As for James Williams of the Walnut Tree Press—Ah, the Walnut Tree was the name of our beautiful ancient pub at Aldington, where I am proud to be the only American honorary member of the Aldington, Buffington & Hurst Ex-Servicemen's

Club. James Williams . . . ha. You never saw
such a fine Newfoundland dog in your life! He
belonged to Bill Williams the publican.

The American Ambition . . . this was supposedly brought out by World, as they were my
publishers at the time. But William Dogg, the
author, bless him, on whatever white Heavenly
beach he is now trotting—He was with us in
1960 when I wrote *If the South Had Won the
Civil War*, and contentedly for years after that.
Since 30 September, 1965, he is with us no
longer. He was our family Bill Dog. I would still
describe him as "a sensitive pundit and philosopher of our own time."

Someone asked me why I
chose to include *If the South Had Won the Civil
War* in this volume. "It's already listed in your
series of published works, in the front matter
of *Spirit Lake* . . . listed in your biographical
sketch in *Who's Who*." Aye, true. But that was a
paperback edition only, published by Bantam.
The story has never appeared between hard

covers until now. There are scads of people who never read *Look* magazine, and other scads who never open a "pocket book." I wanted those readers to know this story. Fiction it is, but—

Now, let's just suppose. . . .